Sensory Trauma:

autism, sensory difference

and the daily experience of fear

Dr R Fulton (Autism Wellbeing CIC)

E Reardon (University of Wales Trinity Saint David, Institute of Management and Health)

K Richardson (Hywel Dda University Health Board, NHS Wales)

Dr R Jones (Anglia Ruskin University, Department of Psychology, Faculty of Science and Engineering)

We are a writing team of mixed neurologies including autism, dyslexia and dyspraxia. Our backgrounds are in health care, advocacy, social care and education. We are all Directors of Autism Wellbeing CIC, a not-for-profit social enterprise that works alongside autistic people primarily in south-west Wales (UK).

Corresponding author: Dr R Fulton (rorie@autismwellbeing.org.uk)

AUTISM WELLBEING PRESS

ISBN: 9798688437140

DEDICATION

We would like to thank Rose, George and Boj for their patience and
support over the past six months.
(KR and RF)

Thank you Mal for all of your support. (ER)

Autism Wellbeing would like to dedicate this position paper to all the
autistic people who do not have a voice or who go unheard, in the hope
that the world will become less traumatic as we become listened to and
understood.

Sensory Trauma:

autism, sensory difference

and the daily experience of fear

I used to just think I was a different species. You learn in school by copying. I'm quite good at that, I have high functioning social masking skills, which is great, until you run out of beans. So every time you or anyone else does something, it makes an action that's part of an interaction that has along with it what's called an affect. What's required to integrate socially is to be able to meet that affect. And that becomes progressively harder until I can't, I just can't. Someone can be being really nice and then the voices become pain ... like an assault. And I just have to say: "I can't do words any more". And then I stop being so fun to be around. I wouldn't voluntarily be that "un-nice". But you just sometimes have to intervene to make the pressing requirements of that social interaction go away. You can make it work if you just seclude yourself for a bit. Most people know if I just sit in the corner and do stuff online it's not because I hate them. It's just because I cannot deal with the feelings[1].

Introduction

Autistic people[2] use their bodies, sounds and words to declare that their sensory experience is different to that of non-autistic people. Accounts of autistic sensory experience can be found in two genres of "sensory writing" that, whilst ostensibly referring to the same lived experience, appear to run on parallel, if not divergent, tracks[3]. Autistic people, when they recount their sensory experience of the world, use language quite different to that used by autism professionals. Sensory writing by autistic people is, of its nature, self-referential. It may be nuanced and reflective as well as, at times, graphic, shocking and replete with sensory detail. Autistic sensory writing describes the relationship between individual bodies and the world, hence is multifarious. By contrast, sensory writing by autism professionals tends to be siloed by discipline and heavily constrained by the conventions of clinical-academic discourse. Partly on account of these constraints, sensory writing by autism professionals is, for the most part[4], neurocentric[5] and so tends to exclude the relationship between individual autistic bodies and the world. Whilst neurocentric sensory writing has begun to incorporate the testimony of autistic people[6789101112], the perception persists that autistic people somehow lack rhetoricity[131415] and that their testimony is thereby rendered invalid[16]. In this paper, we contrast the autistic and neurocentric genres of sensory writing and seek to reconcile them using the concept of affordances[17]. On this basis, we generate a novel "Sensory Trauma" framework within which to consider the lived experience of autistic people.

Neurocentric Sensory Writing

In neurocentric sensory writing, autistic sensory experience tends to be cast in the scientific language of sensory processing. Examples of such terminology include sensory processing disorder, abnormal sensory response, sensory dysfunction, sensory sensitivity and unusual sensory behaviours. Within sensory processing itself, different processing patterns or styles are identified. Examples here include hyper- or hypo-reactivity to sensory input, unusual interest in sensory aspects of the environment and sensory over- or under-responsivity. Such language, and the parsing of sensory experience that it implies, is employed across autism discourse in academic, clinical and popular representations of autistic sensory experience.

Neurocentric sensory writing is notable for being indexed against a putative norm, what Yergeau refers to as "the non-autistic bodymind"[18]. In characterising sensory processing, descriptors such as disorder, dysfunction, abnormal, unusual and sensitivity imply the existence of an average or typical operation of human sensory processing. Similarly, in characterising sensory processing patterns, descriptors such as hyper- and hypo-reactive, over- and under-responsive, unusual and disorder imply a notionally typical repertoire of human sensory processing patterns. Drawing attention to the normative stance of neurocentric sensory writing is not to deny that autistic people may have difficult sensory experiences, nor to contest a neurological explanation for such difficulties. Rather, we highlight the way in which autism professionals tend to assume that the sense systems of autistic people operate in the same way as their own.

When an autistic person is said to exhibit a hyper-reactive response to, for example, the sound of a door slamming, their response is classified as hyper-reactive because, to the non-autistic autism professional, the sound of a door slamming is quite within the range of what is expectable and acceptable. The autism professional's perception of the sound is thus the putative "norm" against which the autistic person's response is characterised as hyper-reactive. Similarly, an autistic person may be deemed to have unusual sensory behaviours because she persistently touches and rubs objects, edges and surfaces in her environment. Such behaviours are classified by the non-autistic autism professional as unusual sensory behaviours because they are behaviours in which the autistic professional himself does not engage and could not imagine himself engaging.

The normative reflex in neurocentric sensory writing is the same reflex that animates autism discourse itself. Autism discourse orients to a medical model of disability that "primarily figures disability as a problem of individual bodies in need of cure or repair"[19]. Our interest here, however, is not explicitly or primarily to contrast a medical model of disability against a social model but, rather, to create a discursive space in which autistic sensory experience might be pondered free from any normative tilt or filter – that is, where it can be understood as difference rather than deficit. Towards this end, we distance ourselves from conventional definitions of autism and embrace instead an emergent sensorimotor perspective[20] that seeks to understand autism by foregrounding sensorimotor experiences[212223242526] rather than social and communication difficulties.

The Sensorimotor Perspective

The sensorimotor perspective on autism eschews the socially defined focus of traditional views of autism that prioritise the "triad of impairments"[27], proceeding instead from the understanding that "behaviours may not be what they seem"[28]. The sensorimotor perspective asks, what are the sensory and motoric experiences which underpin and motivate the autistic behaviours upon which current systems for identifying, diagnosing and "treating" autism are founded?

Sensorimotor approaches stake out the ground for autism as "a fully embodied experiential"[29] and thereby ask us to redirect our analytical focus away from behaviour in favour of lived experience. In foregrounding sensory experience, we are primarily interested in "neither the individual, not the contents of the individual's head (mind or brain), nor a set of environmental stimuli, but the interaction of person and environment"[30]. Given this analytical focus, we enlist the concept of affordances as an apposite lens through which to consider autistic sensory experience.

The Concept of Affordances

According to Gibson's ecological approach, affordances are the opportunities for perception and action offered by the environment to an individual in relation to their characteristics and capacities:

> "[t]he *affordances* of the environment are what it *offers* the animal, what it *provides* or *furnishes*, either for good or ill. [...]. I mean by it something that refers to both the environment and the animal [...] it implies the complementarity of the animal and the environment. [...]"[31] (original emphasis).

Affordances are neither in the environment nor in the perceiver but instead derive from the relationship between perceiver (individual) and what is perceived (environment). Affordances may be experienced by the perceiver as positive or negative, they are not inferred or deduced but are perceived directly and derive from the interaction of the individual and environment. The perceiver does not perceive or act upon every affordance in their environment, rather, the perception of affordances depends on the particular information in the environment that is picked up by the perceiver. In turn, information pick-up depends on the characteristics and capacities of the perceiver (*eg* perceptual capacity, state of arousal, motor skills, affect) and the nature of the interaction between the perceiver and the environment[32]. From this it follows that an affordance derives from the interaction between a *particular* perceiver and their environment. The affordances that an environment offers to one individual may be quite different from the affordances that the same environment offers to another individual[33].

Loveland proposes three non-exclusive categories of affordance found in the human environment. The categories may be thought of as "layered"[34] in so far as a particular object, person or event simultaneously offers multiple affordances to the human perceiver:

- o *Affordances for physical transactions with the environment* (*eg* walking on, sitting on, holding, squeezing). The perception of this type of affordance allows us to navigate our immediate environment and to determine what we can walk on, sit on, grasp, use as a container and so on.
- o *Specific, culturally selected affordances that reflect preferred but not necessary interactions* (*eg* a colander affords both rinsing salad leaves and wearing as a hat, but the latter is not a preferred affordance).
- o *Social and communicative affordances that reflect the meaning of human activity for other humans* (*eg* symbolic behaviour such as spoken language and writing, as well as non-symbolic behaviour such as facial expression, gesture, body posture and movements, tone of voice and direction of gaze)[35].

In addition to these three categories, we propose the addition of a fourth, that of sensory affordances:

- o *Sensory affordances.* These affordances reflect the availability in the environment (or in the body) of sensory information in all modalities. Sensory affordances may be experienced by the perceiver as positive or negative.

Sensory Affordances

In the context of affordances, autistic experience has, to

date, been considered primarily in terms of the ways in which autistic people fail to perceive or only partially perceive social affordances[363738]. Here, we shift the focus from the social to the sensory. By framing autistic experience in terms of sensory rather than social affordances, we uncouple autistic sensory experience from the normative language used in neurocentric sensory writing. In so doing, our aim is to decentre the "impaired" sociality of autistic people as a putatively objective indicator of their competence and capacities in social interaction. In line with the sensorimotor perspective, we posit instead an autistic sociality[39] characterised not by a series of deficits but by a combination of competences and constraints. In so doing, we make room to consider the role of sensory experience in accounting for such an autistic sociality. We propose that autistic people have a range of social competences and capacities but that the interactive expression of these may be hampered by the ongoing sensory experience of their body in the world.

As Donnellan *et al* observe,

> [d]ifferences in the way [autistic] people are able to use their bodies and focus their attention lead many to assume that a person does not care to participate or communicate and does not desire relationships[40].

By foregrounding the shaping effect that sensory affordances may exert on the ways in which autistic people use (or do not use) their bodies and focus (or do not focus) their attention in social interaction, we gesture towards an autistic sociality that does care to participate and communicate and that does desire relationship. A sensory affordance lens allows us to draw attention to the ways in which autistic sensory experience is indeed different to non-autistic sensory experience. It permits a characterisation of autistic sensory experience as embodied relational difference rather than as embrained sensory deficit. In thus reframing autistic sensory experience, we highlight the salience of the concept of affordances for understanding the lived experience of autistic people and, thereby, for identifying ways in which experiences, trajectories and outcomes for autistic people might be different.

Considering everyday human experience through the lens of affordances, it is clear that two people in the same environment may not perceive or necessarily respond to the same affordances, whether physical, cultural, social or sensory. We can see this at a very basic level when two individuals share an environment but respond to it differently. Imagine two friends who go out for a walk. For one, the temperature is cool and they put on a coat, while for the other the temperature is just right and they keep their coat in their bag. They walk up a hill, one finds it too steep and has to stop to catch their breath, while the other keeps up a brisk pace and waits for their friend at the top. The two friends meet another walker who stops to greet them and inquires where they are headed; one friend stops to chat, the other finds the walker's inquiry intimidating, feels threatened and walks on. Later, the friends find on the path in front of them a half-eaten bar of chocolate; one picks the chocolate bar up, says "what luck!" and starts to eat it. The other is revolted and says "what are you doing? You don't know where it's been!".

What is happening in these scenarios is that each of the two friends is perceiving different affordances in their shared environment and responding each in their own way. The environment they move through on their walk furnishes a range of affordance types – physical (the hill), social (the walker), cultural (the abandoned chocolate bar) and sensory (the temperature). Each friend, embodying their individual characteristics and capacities, picked up their own package of information from the environment, perceived their own particular affordances and responded accordingly. All the time, people are picking up different information from their shared environment, perceiving different affordances and responding to these in their own, individual ways. This is the case at all times and in all places[41], whether the people in a given environment are all autistic, all non-autistic, or some people in the environment are autistic and some are not.

To return to our example of the slamming door, for a non-autistic person, such an event in the environment offers a sensory affordance entailing some level of auditory stimulation. In turn, this auditory stimulation may elicit a response of surprise or annoyance, and this may be mild or more marked, depending on both the volume of the sound and the person's characteristics and capacities at the time. If the person is activated and experiencing high levels of stress, his response might be one of anger or rage; if he is regulated and relaxed, his response might be one of mild surprise or annoyance. He might turn his head momentarily in the direction of the slammed door or simply continue with what he is doing. Whatever his characteristics and capacities, the non-autistic individual has picked up his own unique, we might say bespoke, package of sensory information afforded by the event of the slamming door and responded accordingly. The non-autistic person has his own sensory information pick-up which, in the context of his particular characteristics and capacities, elicits his own response/action. That is to say, we can draw a straight line between sensory information pick-up and the response/action thereby elicited.

For an autistic person in the same environment, the slamming door might offer a quite different sensory affordance and hence elicit a different type of response/action. The slamming door might offer a sensory affordance entailing a level of auditory stimulation that is experienced in the body as auditory pain[42]. The degree of pain might range from mild to severe, depending on both the volume of the sound and the person's characteristics and capacities at the time. Mild auditory pain might elicit a response of consternation or anxiety and the person may cover her ears and grimace, wince or cry out. Moderate auditory pain might elicit a response of alarm or panic and the person may cower in her chair or bite her hand. Severe auditory pain might elicit a response of shock or terror and the person may drop to the floor in the foetal position or physically attack the person next to her. The autistic person has picked up her own, bespoke package of sensory information afforded by the event of the slamming door and, in the context of her particular characteristics and capacities, responded accordingly. The autistic person has her own sensory information pick-up which, in turn, elicits her own, particular response/action. Again, we can draw a straight line between sensory information pick-up and the response/action thereby elicited.

In describing in some detail the potentially different sensory affordances offered to autistic and non-autistic people by the same environment, we note that an autistic person, when they respond to a sensory affordance furnished by their environment, does so in the context of their particular characteristics and capacities and on the basis of their pick-up of a bespoke sensory information package. It is not the case that, in showing a shock/terror response in the scenario above, the autistic person is being hyper-reactive or over-responsive to sensory input. Rather, what has happened is that the person has experienced sudden, severe auditory pain and thereby a potential threat to life. In dropping to the floor in the foetal position or physically attacking the person next to her, she responds in a manner that we may consider commensurate and understandable. Were the non-autistic person in the scenario above to experience comparably sudden and severe auditory pain, he too might drop to the floor in the foetal position or physically attack the person next to him. As Gunilla Gerland relates of the time when she was writing her book *A Real Person: life on the outside*,

> [w]hile I was writing my book it became more obvious to me how logical my behaviour was, that almost every behaviour which was looked upon as

strange or different [...] was in fact very logical. For instance, I had these tantrums when I used to scream, bite, kick and throw things around. And when I was writing about these tantrums it struck me that if you put any non-autistic person in a position where he year after year felt misunderstood, and he himself misinterpreted the world, and had difficulties in communicating this, then he might also start to throw things around[43].

When we consider autistic sensory experience through a sensory affordance lens, a new mode of understanding and responding to autistic experience becomes available. Through such a lens, what we see is not a disordered or abnormal sensory processing system but instead the interaction between the autistic body and its environment – that is, we see the autistic person's lived experience. As Bartmess observes,

> [l]ike all people, autistic people are people with inner experiences who do things for reasons. [...] Our neurological differences mean that our experiences can differ from neurotypical people's experiences, in significant ways. We might look like we're in the same situation as a neurotypical person, yet the situation can be different for us— and our actions need to be responses to the situations we're actually in.[44]

Autistic Life Narratives

Accounts of the lived experience of autistic people may be found in what Rose refers to as autistic life narratives[45]. In reaching for autistic life narratives[46] to provide a window on the lived experience of autistic people, we concur with Miele Rodas when she contends that,

> [b]ecause there is no specific genetic marker, no blood test, no brain scan, no physical test of any kind, the autistic body is inseparable from autistic voice. It is therefore crucial to recognise that there is no way to identify or define autism except through analysis of text: autistic use of verbal language, autistic social conduct, autistic physical expressions[47].

Autistic Life Narratives as *Testimonio*

In turning to autistic life narratives as a means of validating and giving form to the lived experience of autistic people, we challenge key tenets in the ontological politics[48] of autism discourse that cast autistic people as lacking in empathy, intentionality and theory of mind[49]. Recognising with Prendergast that "to be disabled mentally is to be disabled rhetorically"[50], and concurring with Crane, Sesterka and den Houting that "amplifying the voices of the real experts on autism [...] is crucially important"[51], we assert the value and validity of autistic life narratives as a source of knowledge about autistic lives.

Yergeau argues that autistic life narratives contest the framing of autism as a compound of lacks[52], citing Rose's assertion that such narratives "work at a connective and emotional level to resist the pathologisation of difference"[53]. Rose further argues that intertextual references across a significant segment of autistic life narratives[54] confer upon the corpus the status of *testimonio*[55], characterised by Cruz-Malavé as

> [t]he resulting textual or visual product of an individual act of witnessing and/or experiencing an abject social state that is more than individual, that is indeed collective[56].

The phrase "abject social state" may, to some, feel too strong or somehow hyperbolical when used with reference to autistic lives. However, when we consider the course and content of many of those lives – the traumatising experiences, the downward trajectories in adulthood and the negative, often catastrophic outcomes[57][58][59] – the phrase is apposite. Cruz-Malavé states that political or socially marked differences attend the production of *testimonio*, and this is indeed the case for autistic people, whose difference is articulated in terms of their neurological status. As *testimonio*, autistic life narratives relate the "disparate yet cohesive experiences"[60] of autistic people, recounting individual sensory experience which may be taken to elucidate autistic sensory experience more generally.

Autistic sensory writing

Grandin declares succinctly that "[f]ear is the main emotion in autism"[61]. Excerpted from journalism, blogs, websites and life narratives authored by autistic people, the *testimonio* below bears out this assertion.

> My earliest, most powerful memories are sensory. Of things feeling chaotic. Of being terrified of loud noises. Of being terrified of a lot of foods. Of not being listened to in those experiences and then being deemed to be problematic for fighting for my right not to be traumatised. [...] And I feel that, in being labelled as having this triad of deficits, I am in a sense being re-traumatised in still not having my understanding of the world recognised[62].

> So much sensation streams in, rushing into one's body without ever being processed [...]. Swimming through the din of the fractured and the unexpected, one feels as if one were drowning in an ocean [...] without a shore[63].

> Imagine having the acuity of your senses turned up

to 11. Imagine being keenly aware of every single element of your environment, all the time [...]. Imagine that every time you walk out your front door, it is like being forced to walk too close to a wall of spikes that constantly threaten to impale you[64].

Your body reacts to the sensory input in a way that signals danger. [...] Sensory sensitivities can mean that we have the same reaction to eating spaghetti [...] as we do to (hypothetically) eating raw chicken. Beyond simply disliking a food, we feel a physical repulsion – our body reacts as if the food is harmful. It's a natural sensory reaction, but to the "wrong" kind of input[65].

Being sensitive to touch has always made things difficult as it means I can't stand certain textures and I really can't stand being touched [...] It has also made hugging a big issue. I couldn't understand why I couldn't enjoy it and why it made it feel like my skin is crawling to the point where it makes me feel like I want to rip my skin off[66].

Imagine having no choice but to zoom in on life. The trash dumpster whose rancid odors assault you from across the parking lot. [...]. The children screeching at random. [...]. Dogs barking, at that perfect frequency that makes you cringe. [...]. The

[...] feeling of your clothes on your body [...]. It's like a sensory attack. No wait – it *is* a sensory attack. Instant overload, from which there is no escape. [...] But what is one supposed to do when that "fight or flight" old-brain is overactive, due to constant bombardment, and [...] it sees everything and everyone as a threat? It takes a lot of effort and energy to constantly suppress that firm-wiring and "measure up" to society's expectations. It's like we live in a perpetual defence mode every time we leave the boundaries of our sanctuary[67] (original emphasis).

Bright lights, mid-day sun, reflected lights, strobe lights, flickering lights, fluorescent lights; each seemed to sear my eyes. Together, the sharp sounds and the bright lights were more than enough to overload my senses. My head would feel tight, my stomach would churn, and my pulse would run my heart ragged until I found a safety zone[68].

To be just lightly touched appeared to make my nervous system whimper, as if the nerve ends were curling up. If anyone hit on the terrible idea of tickling me, I died. It was so way beyond unbearable unbearableness that I simply *died* – or that's what it felt like[69] (original emphasis).

> Occasionally I lost all sense of perspective. Something would seem monstrously large if coming towards me at speed, or if I was unprepared. Someone suddenly leaning over me could frighten me enormously. I felt something was falling on to me and that I'd be crushed underneath it. I didn't run away or throw myself to one side. The panic was all inside. Help! I'll be squashed. Where am I? Where is my body? What's up and what's down?[70].

The language used in this *testimonio* is powerfully visceral. At the same time, the experiences which these words describe are everyday activities that, on the face of it, have no connection to extreme sensation: eating food, being touched, being hugged, walking down the street, being out in the sunshine, being under fluorescent light, being tickled, someone leaning over you. And yet, if we are to take the words of autistic people at face value, then we must concede and incorporate into our understanding the fact that such everyday activities may, for autistic people, be attended by experiences of terror, danger, assault and attack.

If the language in this *testimonio* is visceral, equally it is the unambiguous language of trauma. Again, this trauma language is being consciously deployed to describe the most mundane of everyday activities. Identifying these accounts as authentic descriptions of lived experience, we contend that this autistic *testimonio* speaks eloquently of sensory trauma. In introducing this concept, we seek not to make the case that all autistic people experience sensory trauma all of the time, nor that all autistic sensory experience is necessarily traumatising. Rather, our aim is to contribute to the theoretical repertoire[71] for thinking about the sensory experience of autistic people across the life course. In considering autistic sensory experience, we are thinking about autistic lives, the day to day experience of living as an autistic person. Given its implication in the ordinary acts of everyday life, it is difficult to avoid the conclusion that, for many autistic people, sensory trauma has been there all along, hiding in plain sight.

Trauma as Affordance

The concept of trauma has a quality of doubleness, often serving to denote an originary event as well as any ensuing states or conditions for which it may be the precipitant[72]. A useful definition is provided by SAMHSA:

> [i]ndividual trauma results from an event, series of events, or set of circumstances that is experienced by an individual as physically or emotionally harmful or life threatening and that has lasting adverse effects on the individual's functioning and mental, physical, social, emotional, or spiritual well-being[73].

There is the event, series of events, or set of circumstances, and there is the effect or impact on the person. Linking event and effect is the person's experience of the event, which has a conditioning effect on whether and to what extent the event is traumatising for the person and hence on the nature and degree of any effect precipitated. The experience of a potentially traumatic event is thus subjective and "[a] particular event may be experienced as traumatic for one individual and not for another"[74]. In this critical sense, the concept of trauma is coterminous with the concept of affordances. Just as trauma may be understood as an affordance, so too may affordances be experienced as traumatic.

Sensory Trauma

Taking sensory trauma to be an affordance, we thereby take it to imply the complementarity of the person and their environment[75]. Ongoing events in the environment generate an evolving flow of sensory information. From the fluctuating totality of this flow, each person in the environment picks up their own bespoke sensory information package and responds according to their characteristics and capacities. The sensory information that autistic people pick up may, as we have seen, elicit a response different to that of other, non-autistic people in the same environment. Below we set out what we consider to be the distinguishing features of sensory trauma, based on personal experience and the first-person testimony of autistic people.

1. *Sensory Trauma may eventuate from the ordinary activities of everyday life*

From the *testimonio* cited above, we have seen that ordinary, everyday events in the environment generate sensory information that, when picked up by autistic people via their sense systems, may be experienced as sensory trauma. A principal distinguishing feature of sensory trauma, therefore, is that the events or circumstances experienced by autistic people as "physically or emotionally harmful or life threatening"[76] may not necessarily be the extreme events typically associated with the experience of trauma – war, natural disaster, violence, abuse and so on. On the contrary, the potentially traumatic events of sensory trauma for autistic people may be found in the commonplace activities of everyday life: having a shower, brushing your teeth, getting dressed, greeting family members, having breakfast and passing your day in the company of other people in different environments.

2. *Sensory Trauma is latent in the environment*

Given the very ordinariness of the events and circumstances from which sensory trauma may eventuate, a second distinguishing feature of sensory trauma is its quality of latency, of sustained potentiality. For autistic people, as for non-autistic people, the social and material environment is inherently unpredictable. For autistic people, however, a corollary is that the potential for sensory trauma inheres in their moment to moment experience of the world. The autistic person is perennially alert to the potential for sensory affordances that they will experience as sensory trauma. To be alert in this sense is not to be "on the lookout for" potentially traumatic events, it means to be physiologically activated – the environment does not offer the autistic person an experience of safety but instead one of threat, with the result that the person remains persistently cued in to the pick-up of potentially traumatising sensory information. Such heightened vigilance is not without its costs, as we see in the section below on the effects of sensory trauma.

3. *Sensory Trauma may be experienced frequently over the course of the day*

In the often busy environments in which autistic people spend their days in the company of others, it is inevitable that the ongoing potentiality of sensory trauma will, at times, be realised – over the course of the day, events will occur that cause the autistic person to experience sensory trauma. As noted above, such events will tend to be characterised by their ordinariness. Think of a typical day at school for an autistic child. Moving about the school to get to their lessons, they may be brushed against or bumped into by their peers. The lunch queue may require sustained close proximity to others. Teachers may demand eye contact or a spoken response to their question, or raise their voice when reprimanding the class. The repeated occurrence of such quotidian events may cause the autistic child to experience sensory trauma frequently over the course of their school day.

4. *Sensory Trauma is unavoidable*

The ordinariness and frequency of the events that may cause sensory trauma mean that, on a day to day basis, sensory trauma is a predictable outcome of normal participation in family and social life. However, exactly when such events might occur is, paradoxically, largely unpredictable. By dint of this unpredictable predictability, sensory trauma cannot be readily avoided by autistic people in the normal unfolding of their days. For autistic people, the expectation, anticipation, experience and effects of sensory trauma are woven inextricably into their days.

5. *Sensory Trauma may go unrecognised or be misidentified*

An event providing an affordance of sensory trauma to an autistic person may be perceived as inconsequential by non-autistic people in the same environment, if perceived by them at all. As Gunilla Gerland declares,

> [t]o the world around me, my behaviour was utterly incomprehensible. [...]. All I knew was that what I did, I did out of necessity, vital necessity. And that in the eyes of the world around me, this aroused no respect[77].

Not only may non-autistic people not respect the autistic person's way of being in the world, it may be that they do not "believe" the autistic person – they do not, in the apparent absence of any "triggering event", accept the autistic person's presentation as genuine. From this, it is a short step to construing the autistic person's presentation as "challenging behaviour" or as pathological. For both the autistic child and the autistic adult, the consequences of their presentation being misunderstood or mislabelled are potentially significant, quite apart from their sensory trauma not being recognised and responded to compassionately. Such consequences may include bullying, loneliness, mental ill health, health-harming behaviours, misdiagnosis, unwarranted medication, unwarranted medical intervention, arrest, imprisonment or sectioning under mental health legislation. For all autistic people, when such outcomes develop and worsen, the acute and long-term consequences of sensory trauma being misunderstood or mislabelled may be not only significant but catastrophic.

The Events of Sensory Trauma

Sensory trauma is seen to be instantiated in discrete external events or circumstances as well as in the ongoing, embodied experience of threat and lack of safety inherent in real-time autistic sensory experience. The discrete external events or circumstances of sensory trauma are likely to be ordinary events and circumstances that may occur on any given day in the person's normal routine – mealtimes, being hugged by a relative, going out into bright sunshine. The following excerpt from a reflective piece by an autistic woman illustrates the real-time dimension of sensory trauma:

> I'm back in my office. It is very noisy as we are on an industrial estate with lorries reversing and

machines [...]. I have answered a few emails but done none of the creative work I need to do. I am hyperalert so can feel the vibrations of all the traffic wobbling my insides about [...]. I can see my desk vibrating so I know I am hyperalert. I always use that as a cue to regulate myself. I have my [tinted] lenses and some regulating smells – both are helpful. I have my [noise-cancelling] headphones but dare not wear them. I am too hyperalert and they make me more anxious in case I miss someone coming in if I have them on. My door is shut but I know that people will knock at some point and I don't know when so I can't relax. Someone will use the loo and the hand dryer that will make a noise and vibration. I really hate vibrations I can't control [...] Someone's fire alarm has just gone off [...]. I feel tense because I don't know when the next interruption will come[78].

How the autistic person experiences sensory trauma will depend on their perceptual, physiological, physical and psychological characteristics and capacities.

The Experience of Sensory Trauma

Sensory differences are one of the earliest emerging markers of infants later diagnosed with autism[7980818283884]. Sensorimotor differences in high risk infants who were subsequently diagnosed as autistic have been observed as early as six months of age[858687]. The experience of sensory trauma may thus begin in the very earliest months of life, if not at birth. Below we consider the experience of sensory trauma in infancy and early childhood and how this may affect the autistic person's way of being in the world as they mature.

Responding to Threat in the Environment

On account of their sensory differences, autistic people perceive fluctuating levels of threat in their environment and, in most environments where they spend their time, may be "in a perpetual defence mode"[88]. As van der Kolk states, "when we look at trauma, we find that bodies and minds behave and react to the world as if under siege"[89]. An individual who perceives threat in their environment will typically respond in one of three ways – fight, flight or freeze. These responses are mediated by the autonomic nervous system (ANS), which we can think of as "the foundation upon which our lived experience is built [...,] the neural platform that is beneath every experience"[90].

The standard model of the ANS describes a two-branch system that operates reciprocally to regulate itself. The sympathetic branch (or sympathetic nervous system [SNS]) prepares us physiologically for action – exercise, energetic play and fight/flight survival responses. The parasympathetic branch (or parasympathetic nervous system [PNS]) functions as a brake on the SNS and prepares us physiologically for rest and relaxation. According to this standard model, we can think of the

SNS as the "on" branch of the ANS and the PNS as the "slow" or "pause" branch[91].

Polyvagal Theory as a Framework for Understanding Trauma

Polyvagal Theory[9293] expands this traditional model of the ANS and proposes that the PNS, rather than being a single branch, is composed of two sub-branches, the dorsal vagus and ventral vagus. Polyvagal Theory provides a useful framework for understanding trauma and is grounded in three organising principles:

o *autonomic hierarchy* – the ANS responds to sensations in the body and information from the environment via three vagal pathways. These pathways are activated hierarchically (from phylogenetically most recent to oldest) and respond to challenges in predictable ways. From most recent to oldest, the pathways and their associated responses are:
  - PNS ventral vagus: social engagement – connection
  - SNS: mobilisation – fight/flight
  - PNS dorsal vagus: immobilisation, collapse, freeze – disconnection.

o *neuroception* – the process via which the ANS evaluates cues of safety, danger and life-threat without requiring awareness[94]. Neuroception can get it wrong, detecting threat when there is none or cues of safety when there is threat (an instance of false affordance[95], see below).

o *co-regulation* – "the mutual regulation of physiological state between individuals"[96]. The capacity to self-regulate is built on ongoing experiences of co-regulation – "[i]t is through reciprocal regulation of our autonomic states that we feel safe to move into connection and create trusting relationships"[97].

Polyvagal Theory proposes that when a person experiences stress as a result of the perception of threat, the body's initial response is to try to deal with the threat by means of the social engagement system (PNS ventral vagus), using social behaviours such as eye contact, vocal intonation, appeasement or negotiation. By means of the social engagement system which it supports, the ventral vagus acts as a brake on sympathetic arousal, slowing the heart rate and lowering blood pressure. If social engagement fails, or if a social engagement response is not relevant because the threat is perceived as physical, the SNS is recruited to mobilise an active survival response encompassing fight/flight behaviours such as hitting, shouting or running away. If SNS activation fails to deal with the perceived threat, the body descends into a physiologically induced freeze state (PNS dorsal vagus) that may be characterised by immobilisation, collapse and disconnection, what Shore refers to as "the escape when there is no escape"[98].

The environments where autistic people spend their days in the company of other people may not provide a reliable, predictable experience of safety – on account of their sensory differences, social interaction tends to afford autistic people more cues of threat than of safety. What this means in terms of their ANS is that their social engagement system may not be reliably available to them over the course of the day. Polyvagal Theory suggests that sensory trauma may thus be experienced in the autistic person's body as fluctuating yet persistent SNS activation or fluctuating yet persistent PNS disconnection (dorsal vagus), or a combination of the two, with the range of accompanying physiological changes that each implies. As Dana observes,

> [w]ithout the ability to inhibit defence responses, the nervous system is in a continual state of activated mobilization [...] or immobilization [...] survival strategies[99].

An autistic person may move from one state to the other a number of times over the course of the day, and may experience states of safety and connection only infrequently, if at all. Dawn Prince-Hughes writes in her autistic life narrative of "the pain and cost, the silent desperation and psychological struggles" she undergoes "every single day"[100].

Sensory Trauma and the Parent's Interaction Style
For autistic infants as for autistic adults, sensory trauma may be afforded by the ordinary events of everyday life – eye contact, eating food, wearing clothes or being kissed or hugged. Whenever the infant perceives negative sensory affordances from these ordinary events of their daily life, their social engagement system may go offline

with the result that they are unable to pick up cues of safety in their environment. Instead, the negative sensory affordance may elicit from the infant an SNS or PNS (dorsal vagal) survival response. Whilst parents will find different ways to regulate their autistic baby, for example by rocking them, pushing them in their pram or taking them for a drive in the car, they may find it difficult to create a consistently regulating environment in which their baby can reliably pick up the cues of safety (in the form of social affordances) they need to in order for their social engagement system to come online. In this way, the early experience of an autistic infant may be shaped by sensory trauma as a result of the negative sensory affordances they perceive in their material and social environment.

When a parent finds it difficult to connect with their autistic child and receives no, low or unexpected feedback, they may modify their style of interacting with the child and become more directive[101][102][103] or hyper-stimulating[104]. In such a scenario, the parent's vocal pitch may rise and their prosody alter, their facial expression may become exaggerated, they may enter further and more frequently into their child's personal space and may become more physical, energetic and vocal in their interactions with the child. For an autistic infant experiencing sensory trauma, such modifications in parental interaction style, inspired by the parent's desire to connect, may paradoxically make it even more difficult, if not impossible, for the infant to connect with their parent. The negative sensory affordances of the parent's more directive interaction style may be experienced by the infant as further sensory trauma, with the result that their social engagement system may go or remain offline.

Equally, when a parent finds it difficult to connect with their autistic child, they may reduce their use of affectionate touch (caressing or kissing the infant)[105]. Temple Grandin recounts how, when she would not return her mother's hugs as an infant, her mother thought, "[i]f Temple doesn't want me, I'll keep my distance"[106]. Here, the infant experiences their mother's intervention (the hug) as dysregulating and rejects it, in turn leading the mother to withhold this type of interaction. An autistic infant's ongoing experience of sensory trauma may thus have a conditioning effect on how their parent relates and responds to them, which in turn may result in a compromised relationship between the two. As Hellendoorn observes,

> [t]he different information pick-up of a person with ASD will not only affect the actions of that person, but also the actions of the other person(s) in the interaction[107].

A third possibility is that the parent, willing to try anything to create a meaningful connection with their baby, oscillates between stimulatory and more detached interaction styles. In all three interaction styles, the parent's only aim and desire is to connect and engage with their baby and provide them with the kind of loving, regulating input they know the baby needs in order to develop optimally. However, the net result for the infant across all three interaction styles may be a curtailed experience of attunement, connection and co-regulation with their parent.

Missing out on Regulating, Growth-promoting Parental Input

From this, it should not be inferred that the parent-autistic infant dyad never experiences such regulating intimacies, rather that such engagements may come to be the exception rather than the rule. Moreover, inconsistent parenting (altering between different interaction styles) may result in weak or lack of secure attachment between infant and parent[108], which in turn may further hamper the development of the infant's capacity for self-regulation and social engagement[109110]. In this way, the autistic child's access to and functioning within "the two social worlds of childhood"[111] – interactions with caregivers and, from around the age of three, interactions with coequal peers – may, from a very early age, be compromised. Despite the parent's very best efforts and intents,

> [t]he infant [...] *experiences* deprivation of growth-promoting parental input even when it is available[112] (original emphasis).

This type of functional deprivation may unfold as follows. The parent, anticipating that their infant's sensory experience will conform to their expectations and to the descriptions of infant behaviour relayed to them by friends and relatives, encounters instead a baby who does not readily accept nurture or play opportunities, a baby who may cry incessantly or appear detached, or who fluctuates between the two. When the parent's nurture and play interventions are met with an SNS or PNS survival response from their baby, it is confusing, upsetting and distressing for the parent. An outcome may be that their interaction style with the infant becomes over-stimulatory, distanced or a mix of the two.

With their parent wrongfooted in this way, the baby will tend to miss out on the experience of consistent, regulating nurture which the parent wants desperately to provide but is unsure how to. Left, effectively, to manage their sensory trauma by themselves, the autistic infant loses reliable, ongoing access to the social and pre-linguistic parental input that they need, and further, loses reliable, ongoing access to potentially regulating parental input that might relieve their sensory trauma.

Repeated and Prolonged Activation of the ANS
We have seen how the experience of sensory trauma may result in the autistic infant losing reliable access to their social engagement system and so fluctuating between states of SNS activation and PNS (dorsal vagal) disconnection. In this context, repeated and prolonged SNS activation or PNS disconnection may, over time and as a function of the brain's use-dependent development, result in a state becoming a trait[113]. What this means in practical terms is an alteration in the threshold activity and reactivity of the autistic infant's stress response

systems, with the result that the infant develops an ANS bias – towards SNS hyperarousal or towards PNS disconnection – in their response to perceived threat:

> [a] traumatized child is often, at baseline, in a state of low-level fear—responding by using either a hyperarousal [SNS] or a dissociative [PNS dorsal vagal] adaptation[114].

Survival Responses in the Absence of Threat

Given this persistent low-level fear, whenever the environment offers a sensory affordance that is perceived as a threat, the autistic child's presentation may change quite quickly to alarm, heightened fear or terror (SNS), or to disengagement, disconnection or immobilisation (PNS dorsal vagal). In such a scenario, the event from which the sensory affordance derives may be benign or neutral, but the child's neuroception, in the context of their altered threshold reactivity, has incorrectly detected threat in the environment and their ANS responds accordingly. In this way, neutral or benign social interaction may be perceived as a threat and so elicit from the autistic child a survival response, in what we would term an instance of false affordance [115]. An outcome is that

> the stress response system activates more frequently and for longer periods than is necessary, like revving a car engine for hours every day[116].

It is important to note that, if the child has developed a PNS (dorsal vagal) bias in their response to perceived threat, their caregiver may have little or no indication that the child is experiencing sensory trauma. As Hahn observes of her own experience as mother to an autistic infant with significant sensory differences,

> I am grateful [...] that my child had a fight-and-flee response under this type of stress and fear. Many children exposed to a chronic source of stress and fear might respond with a freeze response or a submit/appease response. If my child had been in those latter, internalized states, I would not have been alerted to how much fear and stress was happening inside my child's body[117]

Toxic Stress

Toxic stress occurs when an infant or child, lacking a consistent, protective caregiver relationship, is exposed to persistent high levels of stress[118]. This kind of sustained stress response in the functional absence of consistent and effective regulating care may be characteristic of sensory trauma as experienced by autistic infants and young children. Significantly, whilst experience as an adult can change the brain, experience during the critical periods of early childhood actually organises brain systems:

> [t]rauma during infancy and childhood [...] has the potential effect of influencing the permanent organization – and all future functional capabilities – of the child[119].

Toxic stress means that cortisol levels remain elevated for extended periods of time, and this can suppress the immune response and may modify brain architecture in regions that are involved in learning and memory[120]. In addition, toxic stress in infancy and childhood can lead to increased vulnerability to a range of mental and physical health conditions and health-harming behaviours over the life-course, including depression, anxiety, cardiovascular disease, diabetes, stroke, alcoholism and drug abuse[121].

Sensory Trauma and camouflaging
Many autistic people develop "masking" or "passing" strategies in order to cope with difficulties they may encounter in social interaction experiences[122][123][124]. From a sensorimotor perspective, we would consider such difficulties as originating in the person's experience of sensory trauma. Given this context, under the normative pressures implied by social interaction, the autistic person pursues camouflaging strategies at the expense of those they have developed for sensory and emotional self-regulation. By foregoing, in this way, the opportunity to self-regulate, the person may end up sensorily and emotionally dysregulated in settings and situations in which they camouflage. As Christine Condo writes,

> I wish I could shout from the rooftops: *You have no idea how hard I have to work to appear this way!*[125] (original emphasis).

In a recent online study, 70% of autistic adult participants reported that they consistently camouflage[126]. Camouflaging results in "extreme exhaustion and anxiety"[127] and a "sense of lost identity"[128]. Camouflaging has been linked to anxiety and depression[129][130][131] and has been identified as a risk marker for suicidality in autistic adults[132]. In females, camouflaging may lead to missed diagnosis of autism[133] as well as to late or misdiagnosis[134]. Misdiagnosis may, in turn, lead to a range of negative outcomes including unnecessary medication and potentially invasive medical treatment, as well as any negative side effects of such treatment and medication.

The Impact of Sensory Trauma

At the heart of this problematic dynamic is a mismatch of affordances: the autistic infant tends to perceive the negative sensory affordances of their parent's intervention rather than the positive social affordance which the parent intends[135]. The parent, unaware of or not understanding the implications of the infant's sensory experiences and how these might account for the infant's apparently disconnected or rejecting presentation, tends to perceive the negative social affordances of their child's survival response. Mismatched affordances and the sensory trauma and social dislocation which they may occasion or compound are likely to characterise the autistic person's social and communicative interactions as they move through childhood and adolescence and on into adulthood.

The most profound impact of sensory trauma, then, is on the type of information an autistic person picks up from their material and social environment. Sensory trauma may orient the autistic individual to preferentially perceive and respond to the sensory affordances in their environment. This preferential pick-up of sensory information may occur at the expense of relevant social and communicative affordances that the environment simultaneously offers. Tending in this way to miss the social and communicative affordances of human interaction, in particular of parental interaction, the autistic infant may, in the very early months and years of life, lack any meaningful grounding in or entrainment into the various modes and moods of human social interaction. Incompletely or only loosely entrained into the patterns and processes of human social interaction, the autistic child may find social interaction progressively more difficult as, with age, the demands of social interaction increase in tandem with parental, familial and societal expectations to meet such demands in a socially acceptable manner.

Autistic people may thus find social interaction difficult because their information pick-up in any given environment tends to prioritise sensory affordances over social ones. Equally, however, autistic people may find social interaction difficult because those social affordances that are available in the environment tend not to be accessible to them, irrespective of any competing sensory affordance. As Hellendoorn states,

> the differences in perceiving social affordances between people with and without ASD cannot be attributed to the fact that the information is *social per se*, but to the fact that a lot of social

affordances are specified by information that is difficult to pick-up [*sic*] for people with ASD[136] (original emphasis).

Krueger and Maiese have also considered how social interaction might be made difficult for autistic people by the relative inaccessibility of neurotypical social affordances, observing that

> there is evidence that many social difficulties people with ASD face result from the fact that neurotypical norms, expectations, and mental institutions simply aren't adequate to meet the needs or idiosyncratic features of ASD habits of mind[137].

There are two compounding aspects, then: for autistic people, difficulty with social interaction may be occasioned by the preferential pick-up of sensory affordances as well as by the relative inaccessibility of non-autistic social affordances. It is important to emphasise, however, that autistic individuals co-create between and amongst themselves social affordances that are perceivable, positive and meaningful[138][139][140].

Rooted fundamentally in the early and ongoing experience of sensory trauma, these difficulties with social interaction entail impacts that ramify, from the very earliest days of an autistic infant's life, across the various domains of their experience as they mature –

self-concept, self-esteem, mental and physical health, family, friendships, education, employment, relationships and life chances. The ramifying impacts of sensory trauma on the bodies and lives of autistic people are expressed in a range of medium- to long-term outcomes. In this sense, sensory trauma may be readily understood as an adverse childhood experience (ACE[141]). Both sensory trauma and ACEs are characterised by the early experience of toxic stress, and, in addition, the types of negative outcomes for autistic people described in the literature resemble closely those recorded for adults who have experienced multiple ACEs[142].

Directions for future research
What are the kinds of ideas, approaches and interventions that might reduce the ramifying impacts of sensory trauma in the lives of autistic people? On one level, it is a question of generating, over time, a more inclusive and compassionate framing of autistic experience, one that "shift[s] attention from deficits to social participation"[143]. More immediately, there is a need to develop ways of collaborating with autistic people so as to generate strategies for reducing the incidence and impact of sensory trauma and thereby creating openings for greater social and emotional connection.

A new-born infant who subsequently receives a diagnosis of autism may be unable to avoid sensory trauma – given the sensory perceptual apparatus with which she was born, she may have no choice but to submit to sensory trauma and manage as best she can. For such a baby, what might make a difference is knowledge, understanding, preparedness and flexibility on the part of her caregivers – that is, a particular kind of relationship with her caregivers. The same will hold true as the infant develops through childhood and adolescence into adulthood – it is the relationships that autistic people and the non-autistic people alongside them forge together that will make it possible to reduce and manage the impacts of sensory trauma.

In terms of supportive relationships between autistic people and their allies, there exists already a body of work on which to build[144145146147148]. The concept of affordances suggests the possibility of elaborating a novel type of supportive relationship, one based on the co-crafting of social affordances by autistic people and their caregivers and allies[149]. Gallagher has written persuasively of the therapeutic potential of an affordance-based approach, arguing that a variety of physical disabilities and neurological and psychiatric conditions can be understood in terms of changes to the individual's affordance space[150]. In this paper, we have proposed a sensory trauma framework within which to consider autistic experience. As part of this framework, we have elucidated substantive correspondence between the concepts of trauma and affordance. Our hope, in writing this position paper, is to have opened up fruitful avenues for reflection and research.

[1] Love L, (2020). Alleged computer hacker Lauri Love: Living with my autism. Animation produced by Homewood A, O'Leary T and Lam M. Accessed on 16.09.20 at https://www.bbc.co.uk/news/av/uk-54072509

[2] In line with many self-advocates and their allies, in this paper we use identity-first language, hence "autistic person" rather than "person with autism".

[3] Our use here of the term "sensory writing" encompasses the non-text accounts authored by autistic people such as blogs and YouTube films.

4 Exceptions include Donnellan, A. M., Leary, M. R., & Robledo, J. P. (2006). I can't get started: Stress and the role of movement differences in people with autism. In M. G. Baron, J. Groden (Eds.) & G. Groden & L. Lipsitt (Ed.), Stress and coping in autism (p. 205–245). Oxford University Press. Davidson J and Henderson VL, (2010). "Travel in parallel with us for a while": sensory geographies of autism. The Canadian Geographer/Le Geographe Canadien. 54(4). 462-475 https://doi.org/10.1111/j.1541-0064.2010.00309.x . Robledo J, Donnellan AM and Strandt-Conroy K. (2012). An exploration of sensory and movement differences from the perspective of individuals with autism. Frontiers in integrative neuroscience, 6, 107. https://doi.org/10.3389/fnint.2012.00107. De Jaegher H, (2013). Embodiment and sense-making in autism. Frontiers in Integrative Neuroscience 7(15):15 https://doi.org/10.3389/fnint.2013.00015 . Kapp SK, (2013). Empathizing with sensory and movement differences: Moving toward sensitive understanding of autism. Frontiers in Integrative Neuroscience 7:38 https://doi.org/10.3389/fnint.2013.00038 . Donnellan AM, Hill DA and Leary MR, (2013). Rethinking Autism: Implications of Sensory and Movement Differences. Frontiers in Integrative Neuroscience 6:124 https://doi.org/10.3389/fnint.2012.00124 . Delafield-Butt J, Zeedyk S, Harder S, Vaever M and Caldwell P, (2018). Making meaning together: embodied narratives in a case of severe autism. Charlottesville. https://doi.org/10.31234/osf.io/aekd5. Belek B, (2018). Articulating Sensory Sensitivity: From Bodies with Autism to Autistic Bodies. Medical Anthropology 38(1):1-14 https://doi.org/10.1080/01459740.2018.1460750 .

[5] Roberts T, Krueger J and Glackin S, (2019). Psychiatry beyond the brain: externalism, mental health and autistic spectrum disorder. Philosophy, Psychiatry & Psychology 26(3): E-51-E-68.

[6] Brigitte Chamak, Bonniau B, Jaunay E and Cohen D, (2008). What Can We Learn about Autism from Autistic Persons? Psychother Psychosom 2008; 77:271–279 https://doi.org/10.1159/000140086 .

[7] Robledo J, Donnellan AM and Strandt-Conroy K, (2012). An exploration of

sensory and movement differences from the perspective of individuals with Autism. Frontiers in Integrative Neuroscience 6:107 https://dx.doi.org/10.3389%2Ffnint.2012.00107 .

[8] Kirby AV, Dickie VA and Baranek GT, (2014). Sensory experiences of children with autism spectrum disorder: In their own words. Autism 19(3). https://doi.org/10.1177%2F1362361314520756

[9] Conn C, (2015). 'Sensory highs', 'vivid rememberings' and 'interactive stimming': children's play cultures and experiences of friendship in autistic autobiographies. Disability and Society, 30:8, 1192-1206. https://doi.org/10.1080/09687599.2015.1081094

[10] Delafield-Butt J, Zeedyk S, Harder S, Vaever M and Caldwell P, (2018). *Making meaning together: embodied narratives in a case of severe autism.* Charlottesville. https://doi.org/10.31234/osf.io/aekd5

[11] Welch, C. (2019). Embodied, Intelligent and Empathic: Reframing Autism Using Insider Perspectives. PhD thesis. Accessed on 27.06.20 at https://tspace.library.utoronto.ca/bitstream/1807/95959/1/Welch_Christie_201 906_PhD_thesis.pdf

[12] Kapp SK, Steward R, Crane L, Elliott D, Elphick C, Pellicano E and Russell G, (2019). 'People should be allowed to do what they like': Autistic adults' views and experiences of stimming. *Autism, 23,* 1782 - 1792. https://doi.org/10.1177%2F1362361319829628

[13] Smukler D, (2005). Unauthorized Minds: How "Theory of Mind" Theory Misrepresents Autism . Mental Retardation (Intellectual and Developmental Disabilities) 43(1):11-24. https://doi.org/10.1352/0047-6765(2005)43%3C11:UMHTOM%3E2.0.CO;2

[14] Duffy J and Dorner R, (2011). The Pathos of "Mindblindness": autism, science and sadness in "Theory of Mind" narratives. Journal of Literary & Cultural Disability Studies 5(2):201-215.

[15] Yergeau M (2018). Authoring Autism: On Rhetoric and Neurological Queerness. Durham, NC: Duke University Press.

[16] This denial of rhetoricity extends to autistic people's everyday gestures, gesticulations, vocalisations, utterances, communicative contributions and expressions of rejection, refusal, preference and need. See Yergeau M, (2016). Occupying Autism: Rhetoric, Involuntarity, and the Meaning of Autistic Lives. Chapter in P. Block et al. (eds), Occupying Disability: Critical Approaches to Community, Justice, and Decolonizing Disability. pp6-13.

[17] Gibson JJ, (1979). *The ecological approach to visual perception.* Hillsdale NJ. Lawrence Earlbaum Associates Inc..

[18] Yergeau M, (2018). p87.

[19] Yergeau M, (2018). Authoring Autism: On Rhetoric and Neurological Queerness. Durham, NC: Duke University Press. p107.

[20] Savarese RJ, (2013). Moving the field: the sensorimotor perspective on autism (Commentary on "Rethinking autism: implications of sensory and motor differences," an article by Anne Donnellan, David Hill, and Martha Leary). Frontiers in Integrative Neuroscience, 7.

[21] Donnellan AM, Leary MR and Robledo JP (2006). I Can't Get Started: Stress and the Role of Movement Differences in People with Autism. Chapter in Grace Baron M, Groden J, Groden G and Lipsitt LP, (2006). (eds) Stress and Coping in Autism. Oxford. Oxford University Press.

[22] Robledo J, Donnellan AM and Strandt-Conroy K, (2012). An exploration of sensory and movement differences from the perspective of individuals with Autism. Frontiers in Integrative Neuroscience 6:107.

[23] De Jaegher H, (2013). Embodiment and sense-making in autism. Frontiers in Integrative Neuroscience 7(15):15.

[24] Kapp SK, (2013). Empathizing with sensory and movement differences: Moving toward sensitive understanding of autism. Frontiers in Integrative Neuroscience 7:38.

[25] Donnellan AM, Hill DA and Leary MR, (2013). Rethinking Autism: Implications of Sensory and Movement Differences. Frontiers in Integrative Neuroscience 6:124.

[26] Delafield-Butt J, Zeedyk S, Harder S, Vaever M and Caldwell P, (2018). *Making meaning together: embodied narratives in a case of severe autism.* Charlottesville. https://doi.org/10.31234/osf.io/aekd5

[27] Wing L, (1981). Language, social, and cognitive impairments in autism and severe mental retardation. J Autism Dev Disord 11, 31–44 (1981). https://doi.org/10.1007/BF01531339.

[28] Donnellan AM, Hill DA and Leary MR, (2013). Rethinking Autism: Implications of Sensory and Movement Differences. Frontiers in Integrative Neuroscience 6:124. p2.

[29] Yergeau M, (2018). p200.

[30] Loveland K, (2001). Toward an ecological theory of autism. Chapter in Burack JA, Charman T, Yirmiya N and Zelazo PR, (eds). *The development of autism: Perspectives from theory and research.* New Jersey: Erlbaum Press. p6.

[31] Gibson (1979) p127.

[32] Gibson E. J., Pick A. D. (2000). Perceptual Learning and Development: An Ecological Approach. New York. Oxford University Press

[33] Hellendoorn A, (2014). Understanding social engagement in autism: being different in perceiving and sharing affordances. Frontiers in Psychology (5): p1

[34] Loveland (1991) p2.

[35] Categories adapted from *ibid.* p2.

[36] Loveland KA, (1991). Social Affordances and Interaction II: Autism and the Affordances of the Human Environment. Ecological Psychology 3(2): 99-119.

[37] Loveland K, (2001). Toward an ecological theory of autism. Chapter in Burack JA, Charman T, Yirmiya N and Zelazo PR, (eds). *The development of autism: Perspectives from theory and research.* New Jersey: Erlbaum Press.

[38] Hellendoorn A, (2014). Understanding social engagement in autism: being different in perceiving and sharing affordances. Frontiers in Psychology (5).

[39] Ochs E and Solomon O, (2010). Autistic Sociality. ETHOS, Vol. 38, Issue 1, pp. 69–92

[40] Donnellan AM, Hill DA and Leary MR, (2013). Rethinking Autism: Implications of Sensory and Movement Differences. Frontiers in Integrative Neuroscience 6:124. p7.

[41] Gibson JJ, (1979). *The ecological approach to visual perception.* Hillsdale NJ. Lawrence Earlbaum Associates Inc..

[42] Alternatively, the event might provide a different sensory affordance if the autistic person's auditory perception is muted or low, *ie* the person may not perceive the affordance and so not respond at all. It is worth noting that sensory experience that is muted or low may equally be experienced as traumatic, depending on the event, the environmental conditions and the person's characteristics and capacities.

[43] Gerland G, (1997). The Human Condition: my family and other strangers. The Independent newspaper. Accessed at https://www.independent.co.uk/lifestyle/the-human-condition-my-family-and-other-strangers-1235421.html on 03.07.20

[44] Bartmess E, (2018). What Good Representation of Autistic Characters Looks Like, Part I: Interiority and Neurology. Accessed at http://www.thinkingautismguide.com/2018/02/what-good-representation-of-autistic.html on 06.08.20.

[45] Rose I, (2008). Autistic biography or autistic life narrative? Journal of Literary Disability, 2:1, 44-54.

[46] As with the term sensory writing, we stretch "autistic life narratives" here to include non-text accounts authored by autistic people, such as blogs and YouTube films.

[47] Miele Rodas J, (2018). Autistic Disturbances: theorizing autism poetics from the DSM to Robinson Crusoe. U. Michigan Press. Ann Arbor. p11.

[48] Mol A, (2002). The Body Multiple: ontology in medical practice. Duke University Press. Durham, USA. pviii.

[49] For a discussion of the ways in which autism is framed as a compound of "lacks", see Yergeau, (2018). Introduction.

[50] Prendergast C. On the Rhetorics of Mental Disability. Chapter in Embodied Rhetorics: disability in language and aculture. Wilson JC and Lewiecki-Wilson C (eds), (2001). Carbondale, Il. Southern Illinois U. Press. p57. Cited in Price M, (2009). "Her pronouns wax and wane": psychosocial disability, autobiography and counter-diagnosis. J. Literary and Cultural Disability Studies. 3:1.

[51] Crane L, Sesterka A and den Houting J, (2020). Inclusion and Rigor in Qualitative Autism Research: A Response to Van Schalkwyk and Dewinter (2020). Letter to the Editor, 31.07.20. Journal of Autism and Developmental Disorders.

[52] Yergeau M (2018). Authoring Autism: On Rhetoric and Neurological Queerness. Durham, NC: Duke University Press.

[53] Rose I, (2008). Autistic biography or autistic life narrative? Journal of Literary Disability, 2:1. p46.

[54] Consistency across autistic life narratives regarding the significance of sensory experience is also noted by Ian Hacking [Hacking I, (2009). Autistic Autobiography. Philosophical Transactions of the Royal Society of Biological Sciences 364 (1522): 1467–1473] and Joyce Davidson [Davidson J, (2008). Autistic Culture Online: Virtual Communication and Cultural Expression on the Spectrum. Social and Cultural Geography 9 (7): 791–806].

[55] Ibid. p47.

[56] Cruz-Malavé A, (2017). Testimonio. Entry 60 in Vargas DR, Raquel Mirabal N and La Fountain-Stokes L, (eds), (2017). Keywords for Latina/o Studies. New York U. Press. New York. pp228-231.

[57] Steinhausen HC, Mohr Jensen C, Lauritsen MB. A systematic review and meta-analysis of the long-term overall outcome of autism spectrum disorders in adolescence and adulthood. Acta Psychiatr Scand. 2016; 133:445–52

[58] Guan J and Li G, (2017). Injury Mortality in Individuals With Autism American Journal of Public Health 107, 791-793

[59] Hirvikoski T, Mittendorfer-Rutz E, Boman M, Larsson H, Lichtenstein P and Bölte S, (2016). Premature mortality in autism spectrum disorder. The British Journal of Psychiatry (2016). 208, 232–238.

[60] Rose I, (2008). Autistic biography or autistic life narrative? Journal of Literary Disability, 2:1. p48.

[61] Grandin T, (2015). Thinking the Way Animals Do: Unique insights from a person with a singular understanding. Western Horseman, Nov. 1997, pp.140-145. (Updated January 2015). Accessed at https://www.grandin.com/references/thinking.animals.html on 08.07.20

[62] Oneaspiemama, (2018). What I understand autism to be. Oneaspiemama blog. Accessed at https://oneaspiemama.wordpress.com/2018/04/02/what-i-understand-autism-to-be/ on 08.07.20

[63] Prince-Hughes D, (2004). Songs of the Gorilla Nation: my journey through autism. Three Rivers Press. New York.

[64] Condo CM, (2020). 'You don't look autistic': The reality of high-functioning autism. The Washington Post. Accessed on 21.08.20 at https://www.washingtonpost.com/lifestyle/2020/03/03/you-dont-look-autistic-reality-high-functioning-autism/

[65] Kim C, (2014). Musingsofanaspie blog. The difference between a sensory sensitivity and disliking something. Accessed at https://musingsofanaspie.com/2014/01/30/the-difference-between-a-sensory-sensitivity-and-disliking-something/ on 08.07.20.

[66] Lightowler H, (2019). Unrecognised Autism. Chapter in Caldwell P, Bradley E, Gurney J, Heath J, Lightowler H, Richardson K and Swales J, (2019). Responsive Communication: combining attention to sensory issues with using body language (Intensive Interaction) to interact with autistic children and adults. Shoreham by Sea. Pavilion Publishing. p80.

[67] Eartharcher L, (2016). Thesilentwave blog. Perpetual defence mode. Accessed at https://thesilentwaveblog.wordpress.com/2016/11/09/perpetual-defense-mode/ on 08.07.20.

[68] Holliday Willey L, (1999). Pretending to be Normal: living with Asperger's Syndrome. Jessica Kingsley. London. p26.

[69] Gerland G, (1997). A Real Person: life on the outside. Souvenir Press. London. p38.

[70] *Ibid.*: p27-28.

[71] Mol A, (2002). The Body Multiple: ontology in medical practice. Duke University Press. Durham, USA. pviii.

[72] The definition of trauma and of posttraumatic stress disorder have been the subject of considerable debate and controversy in recent years. For an overview, see Pai A, Suris AM and North CS, (2017). Posttraumatic Stress Disorder in the DSM-5: Controversy, Change, and Conceptual Considerations. Behavioral sciences. 7(1), 7. https://doi.org/10.3390/bs7010007

[73] SAMHSA (Substance Abuse and Mental Health Services Administration), (2014). Concept of trauma and guidance for a trauma-informed approach. p6. Accessed at https://store.samhsa.gov/product/SAMHSA-s-Concept-of-Trauma-and-Guidance-for-a-Trauma-Informed-Approach/SMA14-4884 on 10.07.20.

[74] SAMHSA, (2014). p7.

[75] Gibson, (1979). p127.

[76] SAMHSA, (2014). p7.

[77] Gerland G, (1997). P11-12.

[78] AB, personal communication, 30.07.20, unpublished.

[79] Baranek GT, (1999). Autism During Infancy: A Retrospective Video Analysis of Sensory-Motor and Social Behaviors at 9–12 Months of Age. Journal of Autism and Developmental Disorders volume 29/213–224.

[80] Mulligan S and Prudhomme White B, (2012). Sensory and Motor Behaviors of Infant Siblings of Children with and without Autism. American Journal of Occupational Therapy, September/October 2012, Vol. 66, 556-566.

[81] Damiano-Goodwin CR, Woynaroski TG, Simon DM, Ibañez LV, Murias M, Kirby A, Newsom CR, Wallace MT, Stone WL and Cascio CJ, (2018). Developmental sequelae and neurophysiologic substrates of sensory seeking in infant siblings of children with autism spectrum disorder. Developmental Cognitive Neuroscience, 29, 41–53.

[82] Thye M, Bednarz HN, Herringshaw AJ, Sartin EB and Kana RK, (2017). The Impact of Atypical Sensory Processing on Social Impairments in Autism Spectrum Disorder. Developmental Cognitive Neuroscience 29

[83] Terje Falck-Ytter T, Nyström P, Gredebäck G, Gliga T, Bölte S and the EASE Team, (2018). Reduced orienting to audiovisual synchrony in infancy predicts autism diagnosis at 3 years of age. Journal of Child Psychology and Psychiatry, 59 (8) 872-880.

[84] Riva V, Cantiani C, Mornati G, Gallo M, Villa L, Mani E, Saviozzi I, Marino C and Molteni M, (2018). Distinct ERP profiles for auditory processing in infants at-risk for autism and language impairment. Scientific Reports, 8: 715.

[85] Estes A, Zwaigenbaum L, Gu H, St John T, Paterson S, Elison JT, Hazlett H, Botteron K, Dager SR, Schultz RT, Kostopoulos P, Evans A, Dawson G, Eliason J, Alvarez S, Piven J and IBIS network, (2015). Behavioral, cognitive, and adaptive development in infants with autism spectrum disorder in the first 2 years of life. Journal of Neurodevelopmental Disorders, 7(1). Article 24.

[86] Flanagan JE, Landa R, Bhat A and Bauman M, (2012). Head lag in infants at risk of autism: a preliminary study. Am J Occup Ther. September 2012.

[87] Clifford SM, Hudry K, Elsabbagh M, Charman T, Johnson MH and BASIS Team,

(2013). Temperament in the first 2 years of life in infants at high-risk for autism spectrum disorders. J. Autism Dev. Disord. 43, 673–686.

[88] Eartharcher L, (2016). Thesilentwave blog. Perpetual defence mode. Accessed at https://thesilentwaveblog.wordpress.com/2016/11/09/perpetual-defense-mode/ on 08.07.20.

[89] Van der Kolk BA, McFarlane WL and van der Hart O, (2007). History of trauma in psychiatry. In van der Kolk BA, McFarlane AC and Weisaeth L, (eds). Traumatic stress: the effects of overwhelming experience on mind, body, and society (pp. 47–74). New York. The Guilford Press.

[90] Dana D, (2018). The Polyvagal Theory in Therapy: engaging the rhythm of regulation. WW Norton and Co.. New York.

[91] Klain KL and Terrell SJ, (2018). Nurturing Resilience: helping clients move forward from developmental trauma. North Atlantic Books. Berkeley, Ca. p62.

[92] Porges SW, (1995). Orienting in a defensive world: Mammalian modifications of our evolutionary heritage: A Polyvagal Theory. Psychophysiology. 32:301–318.

[93] Porges SW, (2011). The Polyvagal Theory: Neurophysiological Foundations of Emotions, Attachment, Communication and Self-Regulation. WW Norton. New York.

[94] Porges SW, (2017). The Pocket Guide to the Polyvagal Theory. WW Norton. New York.

[95] Glaver, W (1991). Technology Affordances. In Proceedings of CHI'91 (New Orleans, Lousiana, April 28/May 2, 1991). ACM, New York. pp 79-84.

[96] Porges SW, (2017). p9.

[97] Dana D, (2018). p4.

[98] Schore AN, (2014). Early interpersonal neurobiological assessment of attachment and autistic spectrum disorders. Frontiers in Psychology 5 (A1049). p7.

[99] *Ibid.*, p18.

[100] Prince-Hughes D, (2004). p31.

[101] Landry, S. & Loveland, K. (1989). The effect of social context on the functional communication skills of autistic children. Journal of Autism and Developmental Disorders, 19, 283-299.

[102] Wan MW, Green J, Elsabbagh M, Johnson MH, Charman T, Plummer and the BASIS Team, (2012). Parent-infant interaction in infant siblings at risk of autism: A controlled observational study. Research in Developmental Disabilities, 33, 924-932.

[103] Apicella F, Chericoni N, Costanzo V, Baldini S, Billeci L, Cohen D and Muratori F, (2013). Reciprocity in Interaction: A Window on the First Year of Life in Autism. Autism Research and Treatment, 2013. p9.

[104] Saint-Georges C, Mahdhaoui A, Chetouani M, Cassel RS, Laznik MC, Apicella F, Muratori P, Maestro S, Muratori F and Cohen D, (2011). Do parents recognize autistic deviant behavior long before diagnosis? taking into account interaction using computational methods. PLoS One, vol. 6, no. 7, e22393. p11.

[105] Apicella F, Chericoni N, Costanzo V, Baldini S, Billeci L, Cohen D *et al*, (2013). Reciprocity in interaction: a window on the first year of life in autism. Autism Res. Treat. 2013:705895. p8.

[106] Cutler E, (2004). Thorn in my Pocket: Temple Grandin's Mother tells the Family Story. Future Horizons. Arlington, Tx. Cited in Grandin T and Panek R, (2014). The Autistic Brain: exploring the strength of a different kind of mind. Ebury Publishing. London. p8.

[107] Hellendoorn A, (2014). p2.

[108] Bowlby J, (2005). A Secure Base: Clinical Applications of Attachment Theory. Routledge. London.

[109] van der Kolk B, (2005). Developmental Trauma Disorder: towards a rational diagnosis for children with complex trauma histories. Psychiatric Annals, 35:5, May 2005. pp401-408.

[110] Heller L and LaPierre A, (2012). Healing Developmental Trauma. How early trauma affects self-regulation, self-image and the caopacity for relationship. North Atlantic. Berkeley, Ca..

[111] Tomasello M, (2019). Becoming Human: A Theory of Ontogeny. Belknap/Harvard. Cambridge, Mass. p8.

[112] Singletary WM, (2015). An integrative model of autism spectrum disorder: ASD as a neurobiological disorder of experienced environmental deprivation, early life stress and allostatic overload. Neuropsychoanalysis, 17:2, 81-119. p81.

[113] Perry B, Pollard RA, Blaicley TL, Baker WL and Vigilante D, (1995). Childhood Trauma, the Neurobiology of Adaptation, and "Use-dependent" Development of the Brain: How "States" Become "Traits". Infant Mental Health Journal, Vol. 16, No. 4, Winter 1995

[114] *Ibid.*. p274.

[115] Glaver, W (1991). Technology Affordances. In Proceedings of CHI'91 (New Orleans, Lousiana, April 28/May 2, 1991). ACM, New York. pp 79-84.

[116] National Scientific Council on the Developing Child, (2014). Excessive Stress Disrupts the Architecture of the Developing Brain. Center on the Developing Child, Harvard University. Accessed at https://developingchild.harvard.edu/wp-content/uploads/2005/05/Stress_Disrupts_Architecture_Developing_Brain-1.pdf on 07.08.20.

[117] Hahn K, (2018). Sensory Trauma Changes Everything. Webpage. Accessed on 20.09.20 at https://traumautistic.com/2018/07/06/sensory-trauma-changes-everything/amp/

[118] National Scientific Council on the Developing Child, (2014). Excessive Stress Disrupts the Architecture of the Developing Brain. Center on the Developing Child, Harvard University. Accessed on 08.08.20 at https://developingchild.harvard.edu/wp-content/uploads/2005/05/Stress_Disrupts_Architecture_Developing_Brain-1.pdf
[119] Perry *et al*, (1995). p290.

[120] NSCDC, (2014). p3.

[121] *Ibid..* p2. f

[122] Cage E and Troxell-Whitman Z, (2019). Understanding the Reasons, Contexts and Costs of Camouflaging for Autistic Adults. Journal of Autism and Developmental Disorders (2019) 49: 1899–1911.
123 Hull L, Petrides KV, Allison C, Smith P, Baron-Cohen S, Lai MC and Mandy W, (2017). "Putting on My Best Normal": Social Camouflaging in Adults with Autism Spectrum Conditions. Journal of Autism and Developmental Disorders 47(4).
[124] Bargiela et al, (2016).
[125] Condo CM, (2020).
[126] Cage E and Troxell-Whitman Z, (2019).
[127] Hull *et al*, (2019). p2532.
[128] Bargiela et al, (2016).p3288.
[129] Cage E and Troxell-Whitman Z, (2019).
[130] Livingston, L. A., Colvert, E., Social Relationships Study Team , Bolton, P., Happé, F. (2019). Good social skills despite poor theory of mind: Exploring compensation in autism spectrum disorder. Journal of Child Psychology and Psychiatry, 60, 102–110.

[131] Bargiela et al, (2016).
[132] Cassidy S, Bradley L, Shaw R and Baron-Cohen S, (2018). Risk markers for suicidality in autistic adults. Molecular Autism, 9(42), 1–14.
[133] Hull L, Petrides KV and Mandy W, (2020). The Female Autism Phenotype and Camouflaging: a Narrative Review. Rev J Autism Dev Disord.

[134] Lai MC, Lombardo MV, Auyeung B, Chakrabarti B and Baron- Cohen S, (2015). Sex/gender differences and autism: Setting the scene for future research. Journal of the American Academy of Child & Adolescent Psychiatry, 54(1), 11–24.
[135] The pick-up of sensory affordances at the expense of social affordances is noted by Conn in her study of autistic life narratives in which she focused on autistic children's play cultures: "[i]n engaging with toy and non-toy objects, the

process that is described is one of playful engagement with sensory rather than social affordances". Conn C, (2015). p1197.

[136] Hellendoorn A, (2014). p3.

[137] Krueger J and Maiese M, (2018). Mental institutions, habits of mind, and an extended approach to autism. Thaumàzein 6. p28.

[138] Silberman S, (2015). Neurotribes: the legacy of autism and how to think smarter about people who think differently. Avery Publishing. New York.

[139] Komeda H, Kosaka H, Saito DN, Mano Y, Jung M, Fujii T, Yanaka HT, Munesue T, Ishitobi M, Sato M and Okazawa H, (2015). Autistic empathy toward autistic others. Social Cognitive and Affective Neuroscience 10 (2). 145-152.

[140] Schilbach L, (2016). Towards a second-person neuropsychiatry. Phil. Trans. R. Soc. B 371: 20150081.

[141] Felitti VJ, Anda RF, Nordenberg D, Williamson DF, Spitz AM, Edwards V, ... Marks JS. Relationship of childhood abuse and household dysfunction to many of the leading causes of death in adults: The Adverse Childhood Experiences (ACE) Study. American Journal of Preventive Medicine. 1998; 14:245–258.

[142] Hughes K, Bellis MA, Hardcastle KA, Sethi D, Butchart A, Mikton C, Jones L and Dunne MP, (2017). The effect of multiple adverse childhood experiences on health: a systematic review and meta-analysis. Lancet Public Health 2017; 2: e356–66.

[143] Bagatell N, (2007). Orchestrating voices: autism, identity and the power of discourse. Disability and Society. 22:4. 413-426.

[144] Kliewer C and Biklen D, (2007). Enacting Literacy: Local Understanding, Significant Disability, and a New Frame for Educational Opportunity. Teachers College Record 109 (12). 2579-2600.

[145] Amos P, (2013). Rhythm and timing in autism: learning to dance. Frontiers in Integrative Neuroscience. Volume 7. Article 27.

[146] Donellan AM, Hill DA and Leary MR, (2013). Rethinking Autism: Implications of Sensory and Movement Differences. *Disability Studies Quarterly. 30(1).*

[147] Robledo J and Donellan AM, (2016). Supportive Relationships in Autism Spectrum Disorder: Perspectives of Individuals with ASD and Supporters. Behav. Sci., 6, 23.

[148] Delafield-Butt J, Zeedyk S, Harder S, Vaever M and Caldwell P, (2018). Making meaning together: embodied narratives in a case of severe autism. University of Strathclyde Glasgow working paper. Accessed on 22.08.20 at https://pureportal.strath.ac.uk/en/publications/making-meaning-together-embodied-narratives-in-a-case-of-severe-a

[149] Author and Author, in preparation.

[150] Gallagher S, (2018). The Therapeutic Reconstruction of affordances. Res

Philosophica 95(4):719-736.

Made in the USA
Monee, IL
18 June 2021